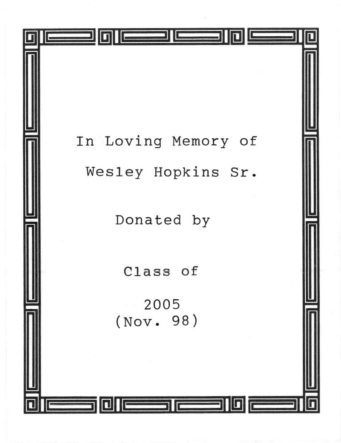

In Loving Memory of

Wesley Hopkins Sr.

Donated by

Class of

2005
(Nov. 98)

Read All About Dogs

SPORTING DOGS

Barbara J. Patten

The Rourke Corporation, Inc.
Vero Beach, Florida 32964

PHOTO CREDITS
Photos courtesy of Corel

Library of Congress Cataloging-in-Publication Data

Patten, Barbara J., 1951-
   Sporting dogs / by Barbara J. Patten.
      p. cm. — (Read all about dogs)
   Includes index.
   Summary: Illustrations and brief text present various breeds of dogs that often are used in hunting birds.
   ISBN 0-86593-460-6
   1. Bird dogs—Juvenile literature. [1. Bird dogs 2. Dogs.]
I. Title II. Series: Patten, Barbara J., 1951- Read all about dogs.
SF428.5.P38—1996   96–23078
                                                     CIP
                                                     AC

Printed in the USA

TABLE OF CONTENTS

THE SPORTING GROUP

Often, with only each other for company, a hunter and a dog set out with one thing in mind: Let's bring home dinner!

Hunting game birds, or birds that people eat, requires the help of special **canines** (KAY nynz), or dogs, that belong to the sporting group.

Pointers, setters, spaniels, and retrievers team up with their masters to hunt wild birds of land and sea.

Let's read all about sporting dogs and learn something special about each breed.

This golden retriever pup will grow into a fine hunting dog.

WEIMARANERS AND VIZSLAS

Sniffing the air, a **Weimaraner** (VY muh rah ner) picks up the scent of a wild bird. Stop! The canine hunter freezes in its tracks.

Lifting a front paw, stiffening its long tail, and staring straight ahead, the dog "points" for its master to the wild bird hiding in the tall grass.

Nicknamed the "gray ghost," Weimaraners come in all shades of gray. They make wonderful pets.

Looking for a wild bird to chase, this Weimaraner enjoys the flowers.

The vizsla is a dependable pointing dog.

Like the Weimaraner, the **vizsla** (VIZH lah) is a "pointer."

Vizsla means "alert" in Hungary, the home of these dogs. The word fits this lively and watchful dog. Although not well known, vizslas make fine family dogs.

GERMAN SHORTHAIRED POINTERS

The **German shorthaired pointer** (JER mun) (SHAWRT HAIRD) (POYN ter) is a favorite with water bird hunters.

Like all pointers, the German shorthaired has a great sense of smell that makes it good at tracking and pointing birds in the field.

Their waterproof coats and webbed feet help German shorthaired pointers swim through rough, cold water to bring back birds.

All action on the field, this sporting dog is happy to curl up by a cozy fire at home.

Their webbed feet make swimming easy for German shorthaired pointers.

COCKER SPANIELS

With a nonstop tail and bright eyes, the **cocker spaniel** (KAHK er) (SPAN yel) gets lots of attention.

These spaniels got the name "cocker" because they are very skilled at hunting birds called woodcocks.

The English cockers have long muzzles that help them retrieve, or bring back, large game birds.

The cheerful American cocker spaniel is smaller that its English cousin, but has bigger eyes. Most cockers have never seen a woodcock, but they are content being a person's loyal, long-eared friend.

Many people choose the American cocker spaniel as a pet because of its long ears.

ENGLISH SETTERS

Long before shotguns, hunters used dogs and nets to trap wild birds for their families' dinners.

The dog's keen nose would catch the smell of a bird in the air and follow it to its hiding place in the bushes. The dog would "set," or silently crouch down, showing the hunter where to drop the net.

English setters are both skilled hunters and loving companions.

The Irish red-and-white setter is a close relation of the red setter.

These alert dogs came to be known as **setters** (SET erz). The English setter is one of these hunters.

Guns have made hunting faster and easier, so today's setters are also trained to point.

IRISH SETTERS

Fun-loving at home and serious on the field, the Irish setter is prized as a hunter and a pet. As hunters, they show skill and energy. As family dogs they are loving and gentle.

Irish setters are known for their shiny reddish-brown fur. Running through the woods, they are sometimes hard to see when their coats blend with the colors of autumn leaves.

Lean and graceful, Irish setters are beautiful to watch hunt.

LABRADOR RETRIEVERS

The **Labrador retriever** (LAB ruh DAWR) (ri TREE ver) is one of the best-loved dogs in the world. They are happy sitting in a field of wild flowers or charging through a rough ocean swell.

"Labs" once sailed with fishermen, earning their keep by picking up fish and broken nets from the icy waters off Newfoundland.

Once ashore, the lab's keen sense of smell often helped capture a wild turkey for dinner.

Labrador retrievers protect their families. They have been known to retrieve, or bring back, children they feel have gone too far into the water.

Labrador retrievers are protectors.

CHESAPEAKE BAY RETRIEVERS

The **Chesapeake Bay retriever** (CHES uh PEEK) (BAY) (ri TREE ver) is a powerful swimming dog. An oily coat and webbed feet allow the Chesapeake to swim through rough, cold seas for hours at a time.

When it brings in a water bird, don't stand too close. With one good shake, the dog will be dry—and you will be soaked.

The water is never too chilly for the Chesapeake Bay retriever.

GOLDEN RETRIEVERS

The only thing better than owning a golden retriever is owning two!

A good-natured sporting dog called the golden retriever is often chosen as a family pet. Besides their pretty warm-colored coats, they are known as good hunters. Golden retrievers can retrieve just as well in water as on land.

THE TEAM OF DOG AND MASTER

For thousands of years, dogs have helped humans hunt for food. They share the success. Without a dog, a hunter would often return empty-handed.

Dogs ask only for a pat on the head that says "well done." Really, they need more—clean water, good food, medical care, and a warm, safe place to sleep. Sporting dogs are like all others in this way.

It is up to us to say "thank you" to our canine friends by always treating them well.

Do you think this black cocker spaniel pup is hoping someone will come out to play?

GLOSSARY

canine (KAY nyn) — of or about dogs; like a dog

Chesapeake Bay retriever (CHES uh PEEK) (BAY) (ri TREE ver) — a hunting dog with a dark brown wavy coat known, for retrieving game from water

cocker spaniel (KAHK er) (SPAN yel) — a breed with long, droopy ears and silky coat, named for the woodcocks it once hunted

German shorthaired pointer (JER mun) (SHAWRT HAIRD) (POYN ter) — a medium to large dog with a short, smooth coat with white marks

labrador retriever (LAB ruh DAWR) (ri TREE ver) — a dog with a short, thick yellow or dark coat used to retrieve game from icy waters

setter (SET er) — a longhaired hunting dog that crouches in a set way to show that game is near

vizsla (VIZH lah) — a medium-sized hunting dog with a short, rust-gold coat

Weimaraner (VY muh rah ner) — a large hunting dog with a smooth gray coat

The Britanny spaniel is catching its breath after a fast rabbit chase.

INDEX